BigTime® Piano

Ragtime & Marches

Level 4

Intermediate

Arranged by

Nancy and Randall Faber

Production: Frank and Gail Hackinson
Production Coordinator: Marilyn Cole
Music Editor: Carol Matz
Cover: Terpstra Design, San Francisco
Engraving: GrayBear Music Company, Hollywood, Florida
Printer: Vicks

FABER
PIANO ADVENTURES®

3042 Creek Drive
Ann Arbor, Michigan 48108

A NOTE TO TEACHERS

BigTime® Piano Ragtime & Marches is a collection of outstanding popular pieces from the early 1900s which is immensely appealing to the intermediate pianist. In addition to being excellent supplementary material, the pieces are useful for recital or other performance.

Not only is **BigTime® Piano Ragtime & Marches** exciting for the student, it is specially formulated for the piano teacher. Pianistic arrangements and carefully edited fingering and pedaling make this book an ideal choice for teachers.

BigTime® Piano Ragtime & Marches is part of the *BigTime® Piano* series arranged by Faber and Faber. "BigTime" designates Level 4 of the *PreTime® Piano to Big-Time® Piano Supplementary Library*. The *BigTime® Piano* is arranged for the intermediate pianist and it marks a significant achievement for the piano student. As the name implies, "BigTime" pieces are designed to be fun, showy, and to inspire enthusiasm and pride in the piano student.

Following are the levels of the supplementary library, which lead from *PreTime®* to *BigTime®*.

PreTime® Piano	(Primer Level)
PlayTime® Piano	(Level 1)
ShowTime® Piano	(Level 2A)
ChordTime® Piano	(Level 2B)
FunTime® Piano	(Level 3A–3B)
BigTime® Piano	(Level 4)

Each level offers books in a variety of styles, making it possible for the teacher to offer stimulating material for every student. For a complimentary detailed listing, e-mail faber@pianoadventures.com or write us at the address below.

Visit **www.PianoAdventures.com**.

Helpful Hints:

1. Pieces can be assigned in any order, according to the student's interest and enthusiasm

2. In both "rags" and marches, rhythm is of prime importance. Stress a steady left haft that does not overpower the right hand melody. Hands-alone practice is helpful.

3. Attention should be given to dynamics, pedaling, and tone to create an artistic performance, just as in "serious" music.

About Ragtime and Marches

The march was very popular with the brass bands and dance bands of the late 1800s and was made even more popular with the success of John Philip Sousa's patriotic marches. Pianists often played arrangements of marches and other popular music. A style developed in which the pianist would spice up the melody of these songs by using a syncopated rhythm (playing between the strong beats), while keeping a steady left hand. This became known as "ragging" the melody, and eventually developed into a style of its own called "Ragtime." (The most famous composer of ragtime music is Scott Joplin, 1868–1917). Ragtime and marches have a number of characteristics in common, including similar harmony, regular phrases, and strongly marked rhythm.

ISBN 978-1-61677-144-7

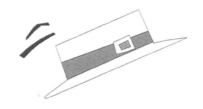

TABLE OF CONTENTS

Champagne Rag 16

Chatterbox Rag 19

"Dill Pickles" Rag 4

The Entertainer 10

Entrance of the Gladiators 22

Funeral March of a Marionette 7

March of the Toys
(from the operetta *Babes in Toyland*) 29

Solace 32

Washington Post March 36

Wild Cherries Rag 26

The Yankee Doodle Boy 14

Dictionary of Musical Terms 41

"Dill Pickles" Rag

CHARLES L. JOHNSON

FF1144

6

Funeral March of a Marionette

CHARLES GOUNOD

8

FF1144

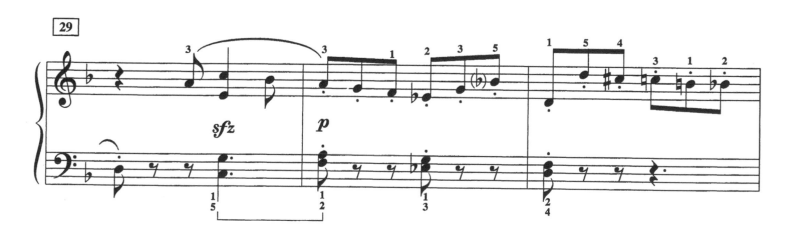

The Entertainer

Not fast (♩ = 112-126)

SCOTT JOPLIN

12

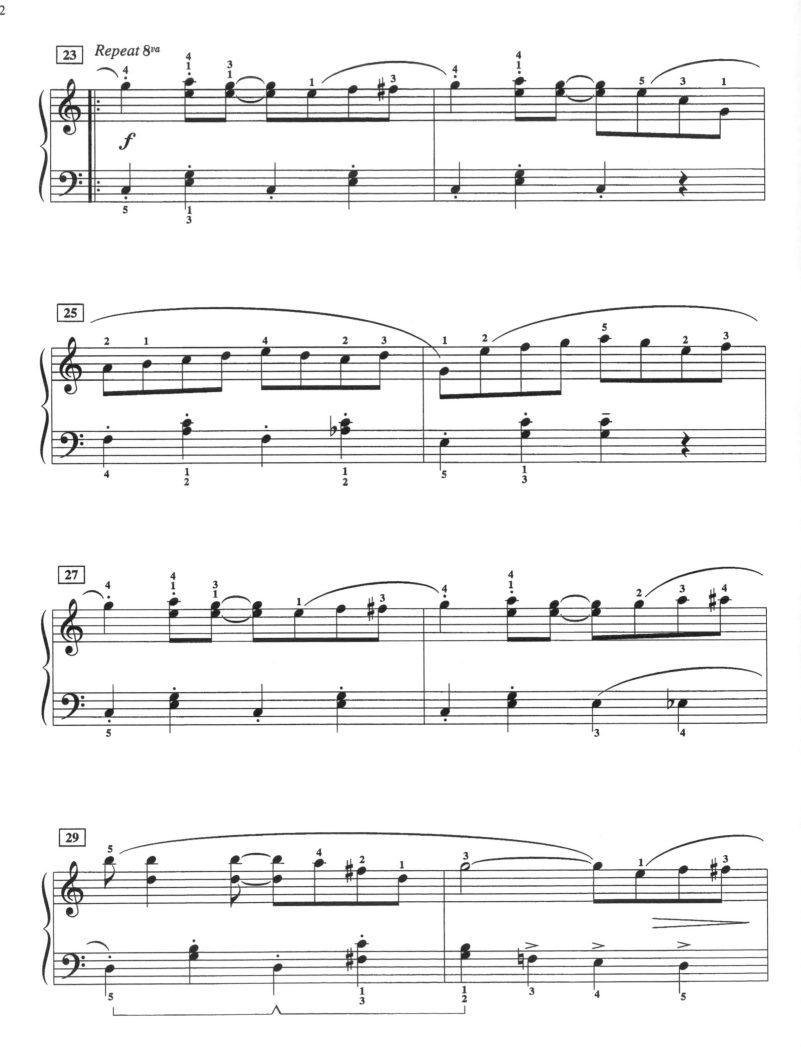

13

FF1144

The Yankee Doodle Boy

Words and Music by
GEORGE M. COHAN

Champagne Rag

JOSEPH F. LAMB

18

Chatterbox Rag

GEORGE BOTSFORD

20

Entrance of the Gladiators

JULIUS FUCÍK

24

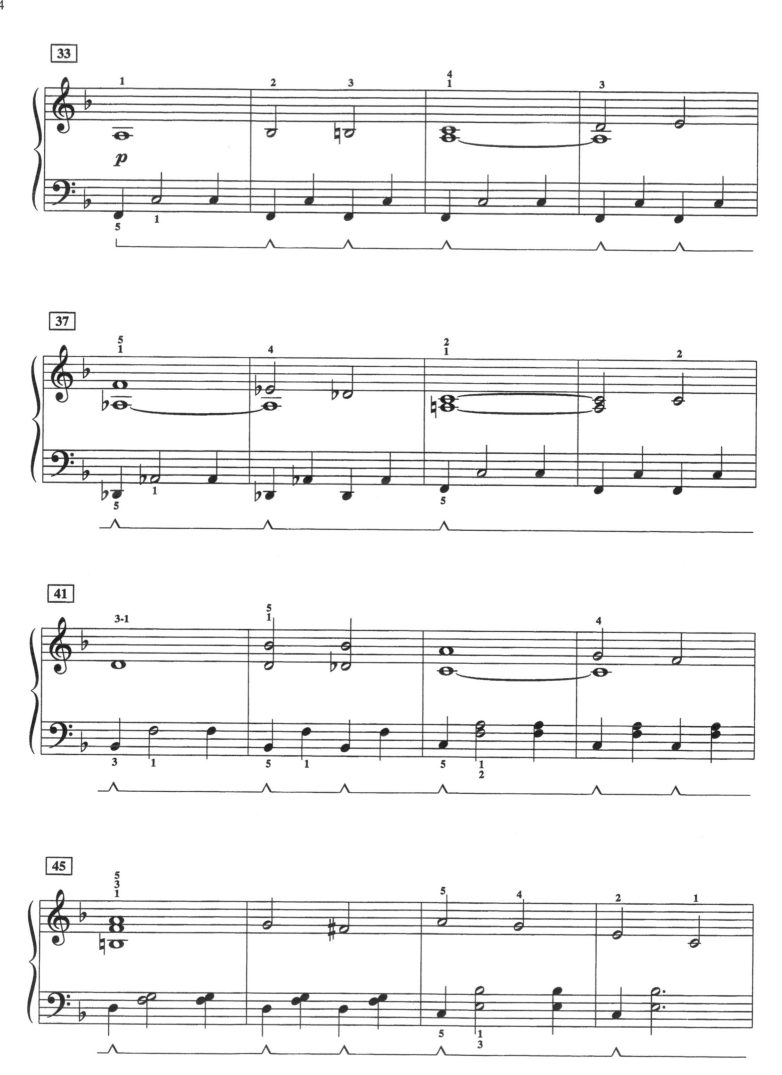

Wild Cherries Rag

TED SNYDER

28

March of the Toys
(from the operetta *Babes in Toyland*)

VICTOR HERBERT

Solace

SCOTT JOPLIN

Very slow march time (♩ = 80-84)

34

FF1144

Washington Post March

JOHN PHILIP SOUSA